Self-Esteem

Methods For Enhancing And Intensifying Your Self-Assurance Abilities For A Lifetime Using Established Strategies

(The Whole Guide To Getting Rid Of Negative Thoughts And Discovering Happiness Inside Yourself)

Clint Warren

TABLE OF CONTENT

Recognizing Each Party's Needs And Wants 1

Spend Some Time Tuning In To Your Inner Thoughts. 37

Self-Talk And Self-Esteem 50

Recognising Yourself, Your Image, And Your Self-Esteem 72

Create Your Affirmations 93

Examples From Real Life: How To Adopt A Growth Mindset 103

Resources And Activities To Promote Kids' Self-Esteem 111

Putting Limits On Things And Saying No 122

Accepting Personal Development 129

Accepting Inner-Directness: Determining Your Natural Strengths 146

Your Tone, Accent, And Pace 153

The Brain And Emotional Growth 157

Recognizing Each Party's Needs And Wants

Every negotiation starts with a complex web of needs and wants that are entwined with motivations, emotions, and priorities. Although it would be easy to concentrate only on our own needs, really fruitful negotiations are the result of a thorough comprehension of the motivations of both sides. This chapter explores the nuances of identifying the needs and desires of both sides, illuminating the reasons why this comprehension is essential to achieving positive results.

The Line That Separates Needs from Wants

It's critical to distinguish between needs and wants first and foremost.

Needs are the unavoidables; they are necessities. Without these fundamental conditions, an agreement might not be possible. For instance, a minimum payment threshold may be necessary in a business contract in order for the agreement to proceed.

Wants are important desires that are not absolute. They give some leeway but still reflect the best case. A wish could be a particular payment schedule or a preferred mode of collaboration inside the same business contract.

Understanding the distinction enables negotiation to be prioritized, guaranteeing the satisfaction of essential needs while making an effort to satisfy as many wants as feasible.

Paying Attention

Active listening is one of the most effective strategies for figuring out another person's needs and desires. This entails hearing words but also fully comprehending the meaning, sentiment, and intention behind them. It necessitates giving it your whole attention, staying silent while the other person speaks, and asking questions when you need clarity. It is possible to pick up on minute cues regarding priorities and deal-breakers by actively listening.

Posing Appropriate Questions

Asking insightful questions might reveal more in-depth information about the desires of the other person in addition to simply listening. Open-ended inquiries like "What are your long-term goals with this agreement?" and "Why is this particular point important to you?" can disclose underlying priorities and motivations.

Seeing Nonverbal Indications

Often, silence speaks louder than words. A person's comfort level, level of real interest, or misgivings can be inferred from their body language, tone of voice, and facial expressions. For example, if a counterpart seems hesitant or uncomfortable about a specific issue,

In Negotiation, Empathy

Knowing what someone needs and desires goes beyond just stating it. Genuine empathy, or putting oneself in the other person's shoes, helps heal wounds and promote trust. Collaborative problem-solving is facilitated when you demonstrate your genuine concern for the needs and goals of the other person.

Verifying and Pondering

Verify your understanding once you think you comprehend the requirements and desires of the other party. In addition to demonstrating to the other person that you have actually listened to them and value their viewpoint, reflecting back on what you have comprehended also serves to establish that you are both on the same page.

Juggling the Interests of the Two Parties

It's important to comprehend the needs and desires of the other person, but it's just as important to remember to take care of yourself. Achieving a successful negotiation involves striking a balance between meeting the fundamental needs of both sides and giving in to as many of their wishes as feasible.

Gaining insight into the requirements and preferences of each side is similar to casting light on the negotiating terrain, exposing the features, obstacles, and routes to success. Deeply appreciating and comprehending the viewpoints of both you and your counterpart sets the stage for a negotiation that is transformative rather than transactional, producing results that are appreciated and satisfying by both parties.

How To Give Yourself An Unwavering Love Bath

The next chapters will explore several approaches to self-love.

Recognize Your Thoughts

Although saying to oneself, "I love myself unconditionally," and indulging in pleasantries are undoubtedly helpful and constructive ways to practice self-love, they are not the first step in accepting who you are and finding inner peace.

This is due to the fact that even though you tell yourself you are loveable on a regular basis, you won't fully accept this advice because it doesn't deal with the root cause of your self-love issues.

Second, because you give credence to self-defeating ideas, you are unable to love who you are. These ideas increase feelings of worthlessness, inadequacy, shame, and embarrassment.

When you give yourself something wonderful on the outside, you might enjoy it for a short while, but soon, you'll hear a loud, annoying voice reminding you how and why you don't deserve it.

That's why nice snacks and meaningless affirmations don't work on you. Understanding your mind and all the beliefs that make you despise yourself is the first step toward practicing self-love. You can say and do anything kind and pleasant for yourself once you've found, comprehended, and begun to doubt the sincerity of these thoughts. This will have a favorable effect on you.

Let's examine some strategies for comprehending and soothing your ideas.

Get Rid Of The Ideas That Cause You To Despise Yourself

Investigating the causes behind your self-hatred may seem scary at first, but if you don't know what is causing these thoughts and why you hate yourself, you will always feel this way and never be able to love yourself.

You will undoubtedly suffer from this, so it is best to examine your ideas carefully right now and identify the root of your self-hatred.

Giving yourself the gift of time—the most valuable gift you could give yourself—will help you comprehend the kinds of ideas that lead to self-hatred. You cannot identify or resolve your problems if you do not make the effort to understand yourself.

Go somewhere quiet and unwind. Drink some juice, go online and watch hilarious movie clips, or do something that will put you at ease right away. After you start to feel somewhat better, pose the dreaded questions to yourself: "Why do I hate myself? What qualities of myself do I dislike that cause me to despise myself? What went wrong that I should be so hard on myself?

Some of us don't love ourselves because we think we're ugly, inadequate, or unsuccessful or because we think we're missing something vital that we believe is necessary for leading a fulfilling life. For others, an underlying sense of guilt and worthlessness could be the cause of their inability to love themselves.

Look for the reason behind your self-loathing right now. Consider the first instance in which you experienced self-loathing or felt undeserving of self-love. Look for the one memory that sets off your self-loathing tendencies.

This could hurt when you do it. It is better to quit right away if the pain is too great rather than forcing yourself to look further into your thoughts. Being patient with oneself is crucial since it's a crucial component of self-love. Only the people you love will you tolerate them. Love yourself with patience and gentleness.

Try this exercise a few more times, and when you finally figure out why, record it in your journal. Keeping this diary secure and recording your daily progress toward self-love will allow you to monitor your progress easily.

It could seem like it's roaring at you if you realize the horrible causes behind your extreme self-hatred. This can overwhelm you and make you despise yourself even more, which is why it's critical to realize that you are perfect. Not you, but your thoughts are the harmful seeds. The ideas are taking over and controlling you.

You wouldn't ever think poorly of yourself if you were in charge of your thoughts, would you? Without a doubt, the answer is no. It's crucial to let you know, though, that you are entirely acceptable and that your views are the only thing that needs to be fixed because you have grown accustomed to thinking in a particular way.

Distract yourself from your thoughts to grasp that. Take time to consider something enjoyable, something that brings you joy or amusement.

You may even put that song on repeat and begin to move to the rhythm. Choose how you want to approach it—visualize it or actually carry it out. Embrace the present and allow yourself to be carefree in this situation.

Ask yourself whether you still feel undeserving of love after you've given yourself over to the moment. It's unlikely that you'll feel ashamed, embarrassed, or undeserving of kindness and consideration. If a certain "perceived" defect was the cause of your inability to love yourself, you would always feel awful, even when you were joyful and amused.

But if you feel wonderful when you dance or are entertained, it's obvious that you're OK and that your destructive and unhelpful thoughts are the only thing to be concerned about.

If putting toxic thoughts to rest helps you feel better, it's a sign that your negative ideas and thoughts about yourself are the source of your self-hatred rather than any flaws you may have in yourself.

Now that you are aware that your thoughts are the cause of your current circumstances, it's important to disprove these negative ideas and realize they are unfounded.

Section 5: Introspective

What are the signs that you are self-aware? Accurately identifying your values, emotions, opinions, strengths, and weaknesses is essential to living a purposeful, trustworthy, and honest life.

To understand other people, you need empathy, and to know yourself, you need self-awareness. When combined, these qualities produce actions that boost your positive influence, create communities and yield outcomes.

So, how can one become a better self-aware person? Let's first dissect the three abilities you must possess in order to comprehend it:

1. To be emotionally aware means to be conscious of your own emotions and how they impact you.

2. Accurate self-evaluation requires awareness of your strengths and limitations.

3. Having a strong sense of self-worth and abilities is a sign of self-confidence.

Our bodily functions and the way we experience our emotions form the basis of our emotional awareness. Seeing the link between your thoughts and actions and how you feel is a sign of being emotionally self-aware.

Since our values and emotions are intimately related, understanding your emotions can help you understand why you feel a particular way about a person or situation.

Through self-evaluation, we can determine the meaning that our actions, skills, and shortcomings have for us. Regular self-evaluation allows people to be self-aware, ask for criticism, learn from their mistakes, and identify areas for improvement. They seek those who can impart knowledge to them and have a growth mindset.

When we let go of our egos and accept who we really are, self-confidence blossoms. When we cease seeking approval from others to validate our own worth, we can only learn something new after that. We gain the humility necessary to acknowledge our shortcomings without punishing or abusing ourselves.

Genuine self-assurance arises from having the ability to objectively assess our strengths and weaknesses. Feeling good about ourselves helps us identify our priorities and let go of unimportant things.

Now that you are aware of the essential abilities, you can attempt the following:

You must first understand your life's narrative and the tale of who you are. This is how we interpret the narrative that directs our behavior and assists us in determining our goals. According to Northwestern University psychology professor Dan McAdams, "The stories we tell ourselves about our lives don't just shape our personalities—they are our personalities."

Consider the people, events, and aspects of your life that have most influenced who you are now. What in the world made you happy the most? Why did you feel uneasy? Which of your accomplishments has sparked your greatest passion? Obtaining this will assist you in discovering more about who you are and what areas you want improvement.

Developing the practice of thinking about oneself every day is the second strategy for increasing self-awareness. You can unwind, practice breathing, go outside, take pleasure in solitude, or jot down notes.

Asking for candid feedback from people you admire or respect is the third strategy. It's possible that while we all have certain opinions about ourselves, we're not the only ones. On the other hand, receiving frank criticism might enable us to recognize new aspects of ourselves that we are blind to. Never forget to follow advice from others.

Finally, discuss your beliefs with your loved ones, friends, and coworkers. Speaking aloud helps solidify abstract concepts like self-awareness and purpose in order to make them more concrete and easier to comprehend. Writing in a journal can assist with this, but talking to someone you can trust about it is preferable.

Harvard Business School professor Bill George contends that a day is not long enough to have a complete understanding of oneself. Rather, it may require years of observation, reflection, and discussion of difficult subjects. However, as time goes on, your perspectives will shift, and you'll discover more opportunities to be authentic and true to who you are, which will ultimately make you happier and more content.

Genuine and self-assured leadership in the workplace, the family room, or the classroom begins with self-awareness. We can't truly know ourselves, follow our interests, or discover our purpose—whatever it may be—unless we examine our fears, hopes, and wants.

An Effective Tool for Self-Development

Everybody can pursue personal improvement as a constant process to enhance their life and realize their full potential. Although there are many ways to improve personally, self-hypnosis is one that is becoming more and more common. For people who want to improve themselves and make positive changes in their lives, this effective and approachable method has a lot to offer.

Explaining Self-Hypnosis

Self-hypnosis is a type of self-induced hypnosis in which the subject induces a hypnotic state in themselves. In this state, self-suggestion can be utilized to favorably affect thoughts, behaviors, and emotions since the mind is very open to it. Self-hypnosis functions similarly to conventional hypnosis. However, it doesn't require the assistance of a third-party hypnotist.

How Does Personal Growth Through Self-Hypnosis Operate?

There are several uses for self-hypnosis that are connected to personal development. The following are some applications for this practice:

Handling Stress and Anxiety: Hypnosis is a useful tool for managing daily stress and for achieving deep relaxation. You can induce a peaceful and serene state of mind by using self-suggestion and imagery.

Enhanced Self-Esteem and Confidence: Mental obstacles and limiting ideas that undermine self-assurance can be eliminated through self-hypnosis. You can raise your self-esteem by using mental retraining and positive affirmations.

Enhancing routines and actions: For those who wish to break undesirable habits like smoking or procrastinating, self-hypnosis can be an invaluable tool. It is possible to refocus the mind to focus on better, more constructive habits.

Development of Personal Skills: Self-hypnosis can be used by anyone with self-development objectives, such as enhancing creativity or learning a new language, to increase focus and learning.

Enhancing interpersonal relationships: Self-hypnosis can be used to improve communication, empathy, and conflict resolution skills, all of which will lead to better interpersonal relationships.

Imagine yourself at your most certain.

Since ancient times, people have utilized visualization—the process of forming an internal picture of a desired result—as a means of fostering personal development. When it comes to body image, women who struggle with poor self-esteem and low confidence might benefit greatly from this strategy.

You may really tap into your inner strength and power by visualizing your most confident self. This can greatly boost your self-assurance and help you develop a more positive body image.

A major advantage of visualization is that it can help us perceive ourselves differently. Even if it's only for a brief instant, we begin to believe it when we see ourselves as self-assured, powerful, and attractive. As we start to see ourselves in a different light and our self-doubt and insecurity start to diminish, this change in perspective can have a significant effect on our self-esteem.

Visualization can also help women face and overcome challenges related to their body image and negative self-talk. They can confront their poor self-perception and replace it with more empowering and positive ideas by visualizing themselves as confident and attractive. When women begin to see themselves as worthy of love and respect regardless of how they look, this perspective change might help them develop a more positive body image.

Women can also connect with their inner selves and access their own personal power through visualization. We can access a powerful and capable part of ourselves when we visualize ourselves as attractive and self-assured. We can then use this strength to go through our daily lives. Women who struggle with low confidence may find that having this inner strength helps them overcome their anxieties and doubts and go on with direction and purpose.

Lastly, visualization can support women in living in the now and concentrating on it. Focusing on our most self-assured selves allows us to completely experience the present moment and all that life has to offer without worrying about the past or the future. Women who struggle with body image issues may find this especially helpful as it allows them to let go of their insecurities and self-doubt and instead concentrate on living their lives and all of the amazing things that come with it.

In summary, women who struggle with poor self-esteem and negative body image might greatly benefit by visualizing their most confident selves. Women can change their viewpoint, get over their critical self-talk, connect with their inner selves, and concentrate on the here and now by visualizing themselves as strong, confident, and attractive. By doing this, individuals will be able to access their own inner strength and cultivate a more positive body image, which will enable them to lead better and more satisfying lives.

Developing the skill of visualization is a fantastic method to take advantage of your mind, which is your most potent tool, alter the way you see yourself, and develop the self-assurance you want. Commence by visualizing your most self-assured self. Imagine something very specific and detailed. How do you look like that? What kind of clothes are you wearing? How are you doing? How do you think, behave, and speak? Give this version of yourself as much time and attention to detail as if you were breathing it into existence.

Exercise for boosting confidence:

Grab a notebook and jot down a thorough synopsis of your most certain self. Don't think about what you're writing for at least ten minutes. Just write. Don't question what you see; just write it down. Go crazy with your creativity!

This is the reason why.

With this activity, you may use your imagination to paint a clear image of how you feel about yourself when you're at your most confident, self-assured, and best. By doing this, you teach your mind to stop concentrating on your flaws and fears and instead concentrate on your advantages and positive traits.

Clarifying your beliefs, objectives, and aspirations can also be achieved by outlining in detail what your most confident self looks like. It helps you to figure out what confidence means to you, what you need to feel confident about yourself, and what actions you can take to get there. Gaining self-awareness, self-acceptance, and self-worth can be facilitated by this clarity.

Additionally, this practice supports the development of a healthy self-image. You begin to believe in yourself and your skills when you picture yourself as assured and self-assured. You gain confidence and become less vulnerable to the damaging effects of other influences, such as the false impressions propagated by the media or the opinions of others.

This workout can also increase your drive and motivation. You're more likely to set realistic goals, make good life choices, and pursue your objectives when you have a clear, self-assured vision of yourself.

Finally, you may strengthen your self-worth, create a good self-image, define your values, become more motivated, and generate a sense of self-assurance by visualizing your most confident self. You may build a solid foundation of assurance and confidence that will help you in all facets of your life by doing this practice on a daily basis.

Be imaginative and start visualizing!

Spend Some Time Tuning In To Your Inner Thoughts.

Regarding the things that happen in their lives, everyone has thoughts and emotions. These sensations and ideas could be upbeat or melancholy. You might use the simple analogy of trying on clothes for a special night out to demonstrate the idea of listening to your inner thoughts. You either shake your head and choose to wear something different after putting on the dress, or you exclaim, "Wow, I look wonderful!" when you glance in the mirror. This is the easiest approach to listening to your inner ideas or intuition when it comes to choosing the best course of action.

On the other hand, we can apply our inner ideas to many positive ends in our daily lives if we are willing to be open to them and receptive to them. Our inner beliefs have the power to help us reach our objectives in life, develop self-confidence, and live better, more fruitful, and more fulfilling lives.

The most valuable resource you possess when it comes to making the right judgments and choices in life is yourself. Our intuition almost never fails us when it comes to telling us what is right or wrong or how to get the best outcomes. All one has to do is trust their gut feeling.

The following are some fundamental methods to begin using your intuition, which is an easy process to begin:

● Try to use your intuition to make decisions regarding less important issues at first to start honing it in the simplest way possible. You may use it, for example, to choose what to have for supper, what movie to watch, or where to eat.

● When it comes to making important judgments and choices, choose a place where you are sure you won't be disturbed since you will find it simpler to tune into yourself and your inner thoughts when you are peaceful. Shut your eyes, inhale deeply several times, and focus exclusively on the work or subject at hand. Notice what answers or thoughts immediately come to mind. This is a practical tactic to adopt.

● When following your intuition, be prepared to admit when you could be mistaken. Even in cases where your intuition is accurate most of the time, it is still possible for you to misinterpret your inner feelings and go wrong. However, you should continue to develop and hone your intuitive sense of what is best for you and learn from the mistakes you make.

● You should avoid adding to the confusion by trying too hard or influencing the response in any way while you are trying to let your inner guidance show through. If you are leaning toward taking one route, there's a significant probability you already know the answer.

The easiest way to encourage your inner guidance to start surfacing when you need it is to adhere to the above-described methods. It will get easier with increased use and reliance. You won't deviate from the road that is ideal for you if you follow your heart and your inner thoughts and feelings. In the song "Always let your conscience be your guide," the animated figure "Jiminy Cricket" counseled his pal Pinocchio. In real life, the same counsel holds true. We only become stuck and unable to make decisions, which ultimately leads us in the wrong direction or to a complete stop when we begin to doubt and lose faith in ourselves.

Gratitude Exercise

It is essential to have a positive outlook because it makes you recognize and value the good things in your life. Here's how to make appreciation a regular part of your day:

1. Gratitude diary: Every day, write down the things for which you are thankful in your gratitude diary. These could be straightforward joys, happy memories, or the support of those you love.

2. Gratitude in the Morning: Begin your day by practicing thankfulness. Make a list of three things for which you are grateful before getting out of bed. This makes the day's vibe upbeat.

3. Express Gratitude: Give them your time and acknowledge their contributions. To demonstrate your gratitude, send thank-you notes, say "I appreciate you" aloud, or carry out deeds of kindness.

4. Mindful Gratitude: Engage in the practice of mindful gratitude by giving your whole attention to the feeling of thankfulness. Savor the thankfulness that you are experiencing right now.

5. Gratitude Rituals: Establish routines that serve as a reminder to be thankful. You may, for instance, thank people before meals or as part of your nightly ritual.

6. Change Your Viewpoint: When presented with obstacles, reinterpret them from an attitude of thankfulness. Instead of concentrating on the challenge, pay attention to the chances and lessons it offers.

Handling Negativity and Stress

A good attitude can be undermined by stress and negativity. In order to develop and preserve a positive outlook, it is imperative that you learn how to successfully handle them. These techniques will assist you in controlling your tension and negativity:

1. Strategies for Reducing Stress: Include stress-reduction strategies in your everyday activities. These could be mindfulness activities, yoga, meditation, or deep breathing techniques.

2. Set Boundaries: To safeguard your mental and emotional health, set up distinct boundaries. Saying no to obligations and circumstances that sap your energy and promote negativity is a valuable skill.

3. Surround Yourself with Positive Energy: Minimize the amount of negative individuals, news, and social media that you come into contact with.

Look for motivational and encouraging materials that make you feel better.

4. Engage in Self-Care: Give self-care activities that encourage relaxation and well-being a top priority. Take part in things you enjoy doing, including hobbies, working out, or going on outdoor excursions.

5. Create Stress-Reduction Positive Affirmations: Craft affirmations that are especially aimed at reducing stress. As in, "I am resilient and calm in the face of stress."

6. Cognitive Restructuring: Disrupt negative thought patterns that exacerbate anxiety and depressive

symptoms. Substitute them with more pragmatic and upbeat views.

7. Seek Support: If you are having trouble coping with stress or negativity, talk to a therapist, family member, or trusted friend. Emotional relief might come from talking about your feelings.

8. Practice Gratitude in Tough Times: During trying times, consciously concentrate on the positive qualities of the circumstance or your life. This can assist you in keeping a cheerful outlook despite hardship.

9. Acquire Stress Reduction Skills: To effectively handle stress, make an investment in learning stress management practices like time

management, problem-solving, and coping strategies.

It takes dedication and practice to maintain a good outlook, which is a lifelong process. It entails restructuring your mental processes, increasing self-awareness, cultivating thankfulness, and controlling stress and negativity skillfully. The benefits of incorporating these tactics into your life are significant, even though it could require some time and work. Your compass can be a positive outlook that directs you toward fulfillment, prosperity, and a happier life. Remember that every day is an opportunity to choose optimism and embrace the transformational potential of a positive mentality as you continue to work on improving your attitude.

Self-Talk And Self-Esteem

When you learn to tune out the critical voice inside of you that keeps you from believing in yourself, your self-esteem increases.

I often talk to myself. Usually, the discussion is between the me that wants to bring me down and the myself that I love. I've come to realize over the years that the latter is typically bogus news, so I try to ignore it much more.

When I make a mistake, I listen to the more optimistic voice so that I may see things more clearly rather than allowing the negative voice to tell me what a failure I am. Instead of going into the

"I'm useless" cycle when doubt starts to sneak in, I remind myself of my advantages.

When I'm feeling down, I try not to lick my emotional wounds and think back on some of my life's accomplishments. I feel more capable and confident when I use this type of self-talk, which gives me a positive sense of self-worth. I've learned to use it regardless of the situation, and you could say that my inner voice is my closest companion.

Everyone has a discussion with themselves, but a lot of us are confined to a loop where we talk badly to someone who believes the worst about ourselves. This critical inner voice is constantly pointing out flaws, shortcomings, and inadequacies. It is a master at it. We ladies are the best at this behavior and are the first to pass judgment on or be critical of ourselves. We are so proficient at it that we don't require input from others. An excellent illustration would be if someone complimented you today on how lovely you looked in your new dress. How do you proceed? You're more likely to respond with something like, "Thanks, but do you think it's too tight?" than with, "Thank you," and call it a day. or "I feel so fat in it, thanks." Being unable to take praise well is not a sign that you're trying to get flattery. It's your self-talk telling you that you don't deserve the praise and that a critical comment would suffice.

The majority of our encounters are shaped by our self-perceptions; therefore, if you exude confidence, you will easily accept compliments or encouraging remarks. However, if you don't have that self-worth, you'll be telling yourself all the time that you're too anything—too short, too overweight, too old, too young, or too anything else—and no amount of encouraging words will change your mind. Your inner critic is in charge, and you believe it when it tells you that you are to anything.

How do you stop this negative self-talk, and where does it originate from? These are the specific questions I want to address in this chapter since your sense of self-worth is closely related to the things you tell yourself. Negative self-talk is a poisonous arrow that seeks to undermine positive self-talk if self-esteem is the capacity to feel good about oneself. Its goal is to pop your bubble, and for the most part, it succeeds in doing so.

You may be low in self-esteem for a multitude of reasons, some of which have to do with your upbringing. It's possible that you had strict parents who never expressed satisfaction with your actions or grades, making you feel unworthy. It's possible that you had inattentive teachers who didn't support or foster your growth in confidence.

Perhaps you were the victim of abuse or a terrible event that left you feeling helpless and unable to take charge of your life. Your self-esteem may have suffered even though you were raised in a loving home if you experienced a setback later in life, like failing a significant exam or losing your job. It could be that you were in a romantic relationship that ended with you feeling taken advantage of or rejected.

As I say, there are countless factors that could have influenced how you feel about yourself right now. It will be helpful if you take some time to consider anything that you believe influenced your degree of confidence and self-worth as a child.

It's likely that you already have a great idea, but if not, proceed cautiously. It's also okay if something comes up that you can't handle at this time. This process may take some time, but it is vital if you want to eventually get rid of any baggage from your past that is weighing down your present and future.

Most experts say that around half of our personality comes from our gene pool, and life events serve to create the other half. This suggests that at least 50% of who you are is malleable and may be altered by how you manage life. Basically, you begin with a label of yourself, such as 'I'm the weak one in the family,' and then you work at fitting your experiences into that mold.

This is because your brain works best when it can organize everything into clearly defined boxes, so the more you tell yourself you are weak, the more you will seek to reinforce that fact. Of course, it works both ways. If you were constantly hailed as 'the bright kid,' then your brain will try to justify that label, too, whenever it can.

I am sure that you can recall very clearly a negative comment made about you ten years ago, yet have great difficulty bringing to mind something positive that you heard in a similar scenario.

No doubt, when your first boyfriend told you that you were fat, that comment was etched into your memory, while you can't remember being told by your second boyfriend that he loves how curvy you are. This has got to do with a thing called negative bias, and if we were more aware of it, we could make our lives a whole lot easier.

When you find yourself fixating on an ill-spoken remark by a friend or keep going over and over your mistakes in your head, it's because negative events impact our brains more than positive ones do. The fancy term for this is positive-negative asymmetry, which basically means that we tend to dwell more on the bad than the good. This explains why it is so difficult for many people to overcome past traumas or forget unpleasant experiences.

It's a human trait, so you don't have to feel bad about it, but it's refreshing to know that we can work on overturning it and focus more on positive experiences rather than negative ones. It all begins when we pay too much attention to these negative soundbites instead of putting them into a realistic and healthy context.

You know that negative bias is controlling your life when you can relate to the following examples:

You were supposed to pick up your partner's dry cleaning on the way home but forgot. You feel terrible and remind yourself how unreliable you are and wonder what he/she sees in you.

You have a row with your best friend and, afterward, go over all her flaws rather than focus on her positive qualities and remember how much she means to you.

You receive your annual job appraisal, and although it's great overall, there are one or two remarks about areas that you need to work on. You fixate on those remarks and go home feeling upset and deflated.

Your personal trainer tells you that you need to work more on your abs. You take this as meaning you are imperfect, flabby, and never going to get that fabulous beach body, no matter how hard you try.

Mission Statement

So, write down your goal in your diary. But you need to include the why and the what: what is motivating you and what you will feel when it is accomplished. It needs to be in accordance with your core values.

Examples may be: "I will lose weight so that I can be healthy and happy in my body and live life fully."

"I will spend more time studying for my course and less time watching TV and surfing the net because learning about my subject makes me feel empowered and positive and will let me create the future I want."

Setting down your goal in written form will help crystallize it in your mind, focus your energy, and ultimately boost your willpower.

Your Support Network

We all need support and encouragement in our lives. Particularly when we embark on something challenging that we know will tax us and where perhaps we have lapsed before, this is where a support network will come in useful. We need people around us to support, help, and encourage us and, most importantly, to reassure and motivate us when we lapse.

It's a good idea to tell a select group of people that you have a goal or an ambition. How much you tell them is up to you. But you have to be a little careful in how you go about it.

If you are going to tell someone, make sure it's someone who has your best interests at heart. Avoid negative or jealous people at all costs. Some people have their own issues and neuroses to deal with and will actually resent your success or even secretly wish for your failure! To see another fail can sometimes provide people with validation and assurance that they are not so bad themselves. So ask yourself how well you know this person, what their personality is, whether they have a jealous streak, and whether they will really encourage you or do you down if you stumble.

A good idea would be to find a trusted friend who is prepared to emotionally (and maybe practically) invest in your ultimate success and arrange to "check in" with them at the end of every month, for example. Then, the two of you can go through a checklist of your accomplishments, setbacks, and future plans. Remember that human beings are social, not solitary creatures, so the feeling of not being alone and of having support around you will boost your willpower.

Another good idea would be to initiate contact with someone you find inspiring. Perhaps on a forum or blog, or maybe just someone you admire. Sometimes, the anonymity of the internet or a forum can take the pressure off you.

Just remember: avoid negative people at all costs. People-pleasers have less self-control! So choose your supporters very carefully.

In situations where we are confronted with divergent viewpoints, it might be beneficial to discuss and identify a compromise. This can be achieved by asking people for what we need while also keeping their needs in mind. A relationship becomes unbalanced when one party's needs take precedence over the other's. We feel abused if we have to constantly change to fit their desires. They feel abused if they constantly adjust to our wishes. Stability in the relationship is brought about by a balance between the two parties.

Trying to please people is not the same as being respectful of their desires. People will never truly be satisfied with us until they mentally participate in it. Therefore, it is not a guarantee that the other person would return our love and affection even if we are more invested in the relationship than they are. We require participation from both parties in a relationship. It is not possible for one person to manage the connection. Expectations from our adjustments must, therefore, be established accordingly.

Possessing Self-Assurance

Overadjusting to others shapes their opinion of you and may lead to increased expectations of adjustment from you. As a result, adjustments must be made moderately and in tandem with ongoing observation of the effects. You regain your power and attract people who are drawn to you when you don't care what other people think.

Individuals who resemble them or someone they aspire to be are liked by others. It's normal for me to like someone who seems at ease if I'm feeling nervous. I could also be curious about what makes him/her so laid back because, on some level, I wish I had that trait. It's not so much that we chase after people as it is the energy they radiate, something we desire and they possess. People who are content with who they are and do not get sucked into what other people think of them can be a pleasure to be around. That's how we can cultivate a positive self-image—by not pushing ourselves too much! Not very logical, is it?

Your confidence skyrockets when you accomplish your goals without attempting to manipulate others. Both you and other people sense it!

The benefits of projecting a positive public image are numerous. We receive invitations to socialize with more people, promotions and benefits at work, and assistance in coexisting with others in our ecosystems. But the issues arise when this constructed image diverges significantly from our true selves and, regrettably, becomes even more significant. It wears you out because maintaining that self-created image requires a lot of energy.

There are simpler methods to project a positive image automatically. For example, we can show others that we are kind and empathetic, which can help us project a positive image without even trying. It is important to take precautions to make sure we cultivate these traits authentically on a personality level rather than flimsily with the intention of taking advantage of people. If that's the case, eventually, people will notice it. Because of our positive reputation, any relationships that might have arisen will be doomed, and empathy-based behavior will be seen with suspicion.

Thus, how can we simply project a positive image while being confident in who we are and unafraid of others? All of this will be covered in detail in the parts that follow. Let's begin by comprehending how we construct the reality we perceive and the steps we may take to change it to our advantage.

Recognising Yourself, Your Image, And Your Self-Esteem

Self-Concept vs. Self-Esteem

The phrase "self-concept" simply describes how we see ourselves. Our understanding is developed through a variety of interactions with significant individuals in our lives. Our perception of our own behavior, skills, and unique qualities is called our self-concept. Our self-concept includes ideas like "I'm a good listener" or "I'm a kind person."

The way we see ourselves is crucial because it influences our behavior, beliefs, and motives. It affects our self-perception as well, including our sense of worth and competence for particular tasks.

When we're young and still figuring out who we are and what we want to become, our self-concept is particularly flexible. Our views of ourselves are far more accurate and structured as we get older and discover more about who we are and what matters to us. Self-concept is, at its most basic level, an amalgam of beliefs about oneself and other people's responses. It responds to the query, "Who am I?"

Self-concept is made up of three different parts:

Idealized self: Your ideal self is the person you aspire to become. The qualities or attributes you wish to have are present in this version of yourself. It's the version of yourself that you would have if all went according to plan.

Self-perception: Your current self-perception is known as your self-image. Your self-image is influenced by your social roles, psychological characteristics, and physical attributes.

Self-worth: How much you like, accept, and value yourself is a measure of your self-esteem. Your self-esteem can be affected by a number of factors, such as how you compare to others, how you are perceived by others, and where you stand in society.

Our relationships with other people influence how we view ourselves. Our sense of self-identity is influenced by the people in our lives, the tales we read and hear, and our close friends and family.

Self-Esteem vs. Self-Image

Since self-image affects confidence and self-esteem, self-esteem and self-image are intricately intertwined.

Self-image is different from self-esteem in that it refers to the mental picture you have of your own appearance and conduct or how you "see" yourself. It has to do with how you think other people see you. Self-esteem is your perception of yourself and is primarily based on the kind of person you think you are.

Self-esteem has many facets, one of which is self-image. Low self-esteem is a result of having a bad self-image. Positive self-perception makes one feel better about oneself, which raises self-esteem.

Reality does not exist from your perspective. It's actually your own perception of reality. Your mind filters and colors everything according to your beliefs and ideals.

Even though you may believe that you are kind, others might not agree. Some people may think a specific hat suits you well or gives you an air of sophistication, even though you think it looks ridiculous on you. Your behavior, beliefs, and relationships with others are all influenced by your self-perception, which makes it crucial.

People's reactions to you are influenced by your aura and can be either favorable or negative. Your degree of confidence in relationships is a function of your self-esteem. You can actually start to feel fatigued if you think other people think you're exhausted. If you think you look amazing, you will be happier and feel like you can take on the world!

Your image is shaped by your views and personal thoughts, which might occasionally become hazy. A negative self-image might make you very critical of yourself and make it easier for you to take nasty remarks from other people. This can easily develop into self-defeating dialogue. Put an end to any negative self-talk you observe in your life and take immediate action. Change it out for more uplifting ideas and statements. The options that will become available to you will astound you.

It's as easy as getting dressed in the morning and focusing on yourself in the mirror. You'll project a positive picture of yourself and show others that you're confident in your appearance if you think you look beautiful and enjoy the person staring back at you. Someone who thinks you don't look good will be hard to believe, but someone who says you make them gasp will have your full faith.

In the same manner, you tend to seem awkward and highlight your weaknesses when you're not comfortable with who you are. When someone tells you that you don't look good, you'll believe them quickly, and when someone tells you that you look fantastic, you won't believe them as much.

That's all there is to it; your self-image is entirely a product of your attitude. We've talked about the differences between self-esteem and self-image, and you now know how to start enhancing your self-image, which will raise your self-esteem.

Chapter 3: Continual Education for Economic Development Within "Think Rich, Grow Rich: Building a Mindset for Wealth Creation," the chapter "Lifelong Learning for Financial Growth" shines brightly as a source of unending empowerment. This chapter takes us on a trip that goes beyond the concept of static knowledge and into the dynamic field of ongoing education. We examine the transforming power of learning and adjusting.

1. The Value of Ongoing Education

Unwavering devotion to learning—a commitment that goes beyond formal education—is at the core of financial progress. This section reveals the importance of ongoing education in developing a flexible and resilient attitude. We explore the experiences of those who understand that pursuing riches is a path characterized by flexibility, creativity, and a never-ending search for understanding. By means of their experiences, we shed light on the reality that education is a lifelong process that enhances all aspects of our existence and is not limited to the classroom.

2. Investigating Uncharted Territory

"Think Rich, Grow Rich" is more than just a catchphrase; it's a concept that grows when new opportunities are explored. In this episode, we embark on a voyage of curiosity, venturing into unknown waters in search of prospects that defy our present comprehension. We explore the art of being curious in unlikely places, accepting unusual viewpoints, and having the courage to try new things. We discover that when we broaden our intellectual horizons, the path to financial success is rewritten via the stories of those who dared to explore new territories.

Table of Contents Chapter 3 Overview: Changing with the Market The threads of market trends weave a dynamic tapestry that is the financial landscape. In this section, we explain how learning is essential for adjusting to the ups and downs of market dynamics. We examine the skill of tracking, evaluating, and reacting to the changes that influence markets and sectors of the economy. Through an examination of the stories of individuals who have persevered through shifting circumstances, we reveal the knowledge that a lifelong learning-focused mind can serve as a compass to guide financial pursuits toward fruitful outcomes.

To sum up, "Lifelong Learning for Financial Growth" is more than simply a chapter; it's an epiphany that knowledge, curiosity, and adaptability are the building blocks of wealth growth. Through valuing lifelong learning, venturing into uncharted territory, and adjusting to shifting consumer preferences, we cultivate a mindset that not only imagines wealth but lives it. As we peruse these pages, allow us to take in the message that learning is a dynamic symphony that is inherent in all endeavors toward financial prosperity rather than stagnant.

Chapter 3, Section 3.1: The Significance of Ongoing Education Unwavering devotion to learning—a commitment that goes beyond formal education—is at the core of financial progress. This section reveals the importance of ongoing education in developing a flexible and resilient attitude. We explore the experiences of those who understand that pursuing riches is a path characterized by flexibility, creativity, and a never-ending search for understanding. By means of their experiences, we shed light on the reality that education is a lifelong process that enhances all aspects of our existence and is not limited to the classroom.

Three Easy Steps to Accept Lifelong Learning for Financial Success Step 1: Foster Unwavering Dedication

Make a deliberate decision to learn things outside of the classroom. Realize that your quest for financial success is entwined with your commitment to learning new things. Accept education as a necessary instrument for cultivating a mindset that is flexible and resilient in the face of adversity.

Step 2: Examine Various Sources for Insight Examine the experiences and tales of others who have succeeded financially. Take courage from people who exemplify adaptability, creativity, and the never-ending search for understanding. You can broaden your understanding of how education leads to wealth creation by learning from their experiences, which also gives you insightful new information.

Step 3: Include Education in Everyday Activities. Change the way you view learning from a solitary endeavor to a necessary component of your everyday existence. Accept that learning can come from anything, whether it comes from reading, participating in conversations, or thinking back on your experiences. Realize that learning never ends; rather, it's a journey that, in the end, enhances and transforms every aspect of your life.

Getting Rid of Fear and Doubt

Anxiety and uncertainty can be incapacitating factors when faced with hardship. They undermine our self-assurance and obstruct our advancement. This chapter explores methods for overcoming uncertainty and fear, giving you the strength to overcome hardship with bravery and tenacity.

Recognizing Doubt and Fear

We'll start by discussing the characteristics of fear and doubt, how they appear in our minds and feelings, and how they may affect our capacity to overcome obstacles.

Changing Your Perspective

A crucial tactic for conquering uncertainty and worry is to change your perspective. We'll talk about how to change your mindset so that you see hardship as a chance for personal development rather than a danger.

Getting Over Self-Doubt

Self-doubt is an incredibly powerful enemy. We'll explore strategies to quiet your inner critic, increase your self-assurance, and cultivate steadfast self-belief.

The Bravery to Act

It frequently takes action to overcome uncertainty and fear. We'll discuss the value of making intentional decisions when faced with hardship and how each decision can increase your self-assurance and fortitude.

Understanding fear and doubt and putting this chapter's strategies into practice can help you face adversity with a renewed feeling of courage and a robust attitude that can withstand life's storms.

Seeing Possibilities in Difficulties

Adversity is a teacher in disguise, and there are chances for development, education, and transformation among its difficulties. In this chapter, we'll examine the skill of seizing chances in the face of difficulty, helping you to change your viewpoint and capitalize on obstacles.

Reinterpreting Difficulties

To begin identifying opportunities within obstacles, you must first alter your viewpoint. We'll talk about how altering your perspective on hardship can lead to personal development and transformation.

The Mentality of Growth

Having a growth mentality is crucial when dealing with hardship. We'll explore the idea of a growth mentality, which encourages opportunity and resilience in the face of adversity.

Making a Comeback Out of Setbacks

Failures and setbacks frequently serve as stepping stones to achievement. We'll look at how to use adversity as a fuel for growth, learn from mistakes, and apply these strategies to convert setbacks into comebacks.

Grasping the Positive Elements

There is always a silver lining to a cloud. We'll talk about how to see the good in adversity and turn it to your advantage, even during the most trying circumstances.

Adversity can be turned from a roadblock to a stepping stone by learning to see the opportunities amid difficulties. This will help you face life's storms with hope and the conviction that, even in the worst circumstances, there is always potential for development and progress.

Create Your Affirmations

Affirmations are self-statements used to foster positive thinking and self-confidence. They can enhance your self-assurance and sustain a constructive mental outlook.

Are you familiar with the saying, "repeated exposure to information increases the likelihood of believing it"? Affirmations function by altering the programming of your subconscious mind through the use of positive thoughts. The frequency with which you reiterate an affirmation directly correlates with the probability of developing a belief in it. Engaging in this activity can facilitate the cultivation of a more optimistic perspective on life. Additionally, it is employed to mitigate stress, anxiety, and depression.

Affirmations encompass both broad declarations that one begins the day with, as well as precise words that one recites to oneself in certain circumstances. For instance, if you are experiencing feelings of anxiety and insecurity, you may engage in self-talk such as:

● I possess the ability to conquer any obstacle. ● I possess the strength and capability to overcome any difficulty. ●I am going to seize this opportunity to step outside my comfort zone and transform it into something extraordinary.

Or if you are feeling low and unmotivated, you may tell yourself:

● I possess inherent value and receive affection. ● I am in the company of individuals who hold concern for me. ● I possess the ability to confront the present by addressing each assignment individually. Firstly...

Crucially, affirmations are supported by extensive scientific research spanning several decades. Engaging in the prolonged utilization of affirmations has been scientifically shown to have several benefits, such as reducing stress [9][10], enhancing desired healthy behaviors [11][12], and fostering resilience against feelings of melancholy, loneliness, and frustration [13]. There are numerous advantages to engaging in such a rapid and uncomplicated physical activity.

Guide to Formulating Affirmations:

As you observe and document your inner critic, rephrase the pessimistic remarks into optimistic ones. If the critic expresses feelings of worthlessness, reframe it as "I possess numerous talents and capabilities, and I am determined to employ them in addressing the challenges that are currently causing me frustration."

Subsequently, place these remarks in a location where you can direct your attention towards them for a significant duration at the beginning of each morning. For the majority of individuals, the bathroom mirror serves as a tool for grooming activities such as shaving, brushing teeth, and other morning preparations. Begin by vocalizing them audibly while gazing at a mirror.

For what reason? To familiarize yourself with the reality that expressing positive attributes about oneself will not cause a significant upheaval in the world. Many individuals are instructed to refrain from expressing their excellent attributes in order to avoid being perceived as boastful individuals.

Engaging in this verbal practice will narrow the gap in effectively expressing your desires, requirements, and limits to others in forthcoming situations. Moreover, it compels you to dedicate your complete focus to cultivating these novel ideas rather than allowing them to be superficially addressed amidst the multitude of other concepts occupying your mind. Significantly, it supersedes the thoughts and concerns that one would often contemplate during these morning routines.

As a regular practice in my morning routine, I employ affirmations, and I can personally verify their efficacy as they are both uncomplicated and impactful. I will disclose them at a later point in the book, specifically when I illustrate a typical day in my life, highlighting the three fundamental principles.

Give priority to fulfilling your requirements.

We have briefly discussed Maslow's hierarchy of requirements on a few occasions. In order to prioritize your self-esteem, it is necessary to reduce the importance of other, more pressing requirements. You can enhance your self-esteem by mitigating the deficiencies in your other requirements. As an illustration:

➤Has increased costs made it tougher to keep food on the table? Research methods to decrease expenses, such as utilizing coupons, purchasing items in large quantities, or sharing a trip to the farmer's market with a companion. Check for the presence of any nearby communal gardens. If you lack enthusiasm for gardening, consider offering a trade to a gardener in exchange for something you are capable of providing. Are you a new mother? Investigate the availability of local or state initiatives catering to your specific demographic that provide assistance with formula and diapers.

Indicated by the symbol "➤"Are you concerned about the security situation in your local area? Research methods to fortify your residence and keep a readily accessible record of nearby emergency, non-emergency, and medical contact information. Consider initiating contact with a neighbor and engaging in a discussion to establish a mutually beneficial arrangement for mutual surveillance and support. Are you experiencing feelings of solitude and social disconnection? Engage in a philanthropic endeavor or reestablish communication with long-neglected acquaintances. A brief greeting of "Hi!" It has been a considerable amount of time since we last communicated. The phrase "I was just thinking about you and wanted to reach out" has the potential to reestablish communication and mend any uncomfortable pauses.

This contributes to the enhancement of your self-esteem through at least two mechanisms. Initially, it alleviates anxieties, apprehensions, and the factors that your subconscious employs to prevent you from sleeping at night. Furthermore, achieving success in these difficulties will provide you with a sense of achievement and proficiency. Achieving achievement will lead to further success as you continue to overcome each new hurdle.

Examples From Real Life: How To Adopt A Growth Mindset

The narrative that follows is a true account of our own experiences with youngsters, and it begins,

The life narrative of Dominic O'Brien, the global memory champion, is told below. This guy is a fantastic example of how to overcome personal obstacles and criticism with practice, perseverance, and self-belief to achieve one of the most amazing feats of mental agility in history. This narrative is an excellent illustration of a growth mindset. It also serves as a terrific way to illustrate the idea that intellect is not fixed and that, with enough focus and effort, practically anything is possible.

After learning that Dominic O'Brien had dyslexia at a young age, his teacher told him, "It won't be much in life."

Unsurprisingly, this had a negative impact on his self-esteem, which made him more anxious and reluctant to attend school every day.

The fact that the teacher was literally attempting to talk him out of an educational collapse and was unhappy with his lack of effort and disinterest did not help this.

According to O'Brien, "At that time, my brain felt like a muscle, but I was at risk of atrophy due to permanent relaxation." His circumstances and his attitude toward the school have not changed over the following few years. Actually, things have become worse. "I felt like one of the happiest days of my life," he remarked the day he was about to leave school if he had the choice.

After fifteen years, O'Brien maintained his remarkable mental acuity and won the title of "World Memory Champion" eight times. He made the decision to train himself to memorize everything by sitting down with a deck of cards. What, then, has happened in the past fifteen years that he and his teachers agreed to sit down and test his mental agility in severe ways, sharing the belief that he is nothing?

When O'Brien was thirty years old, his "Travel of Memories" began in 1987. The show featured Clayton Carvero, who could recall any 52-card sequence and had a good recall of the past. O'Brien showed a lot of curiosity. He sat down with a deck of cards and determined that the best way to find out if it was feasible was to do it himself. He wanted to discover how Cabello pulled off this incredible feat.

He discovered that everything was possible for him to achieve if he set his mind to it after learning how to memorize a deck of cards through practice, commitment, and persistent effort. He stated feeling like a new world of opportunity had opened up to him, and he gained confidence and self-esteem that he had never known before.

Growth mindsets have no boundaries, as O'Brien found, and his own experience disproves the notion that intellect is something that is "certain" or something we are born with. Patience, perseverance, and hard effort demonstrate that the least likely people can achieve the most incredible feats.

Real-World Example 2: Promote Self-Evaluation and Draw Attention to Parallels Between Human Labor and Technology

We realized the value of helping kids assess themselves when we came across all of the fascinating findings in this book when my daughter Noah was five years old. This implies that we now intentionally strive to communicate our feelings for children and what is happening to them rather than just concentrating on our feelings for them. Instead, he remarked, "I'm so proud of you," adding, "I must be so proud of you because you've practiced and worked hard." So, we started switching languages. This was always met with my daughter's response of "not that easy" in whatever activity.

After six months of trying this, we started to question whether it was helping our kid and what effect this new language was having. However, she didn't take long to cry. "I'm proud of myself because I've been chosen as the ballerina of the week, and that's all because I practiced hard!" when she got home from ballet. That's what we've desired from the beginning. She not only greatly raised her confidence and sense of self-worth, but she also realized that she had worked extremely hard to get there.

She demonstrated that she recognized how much practice was necessary to achieve a goal and that she fully comprehended what it meant to feel like she was growing. And she will continue to benefit from this significant learning experience for years to come. As for us, we were obviously quite proud of Norr even though we were very careful with our words when we revealed this information to her.

Resources And Activities To Promote Kids' Self-Esteem

Reducing the number of options available to kids early on can aid in decision-making and confidence-building. Although there are usually only two options available, this autonomy will allow them to express their values and sense of self, lessen power struggles and disputes, and make them more receptive to your requests. Because they let kids share responsibility under their own terms rather than take charge, limited options are incredibly successful. It demonstrates your readiness to trust them, lets them feel in charge of the circumstance, acknowledges the importance of their thoughts, and shows them that their feelings are being acknowledged. It is also the best "real world" preparation since it gives kids early decision-making experience by giving them options.

How to reduce the alternatives available to you:

1. Contemplate two possibilities that are either limiting or appropriate for you.

2. Discuss these possibilities with your child before they have a chance to object to your suggestion (i.e. before a power conflict occurs). In order to provide restricted options throughout the day, it is required to substitute limited options (or inquiries, positive and enforceable

comments, etc.) for as many order commands as possible.

3. Request that your child select one of the two options. As an illustration, a) "Have you brushed your teeth yet? Or in fifteen minutes, will you polish it?"

c) "Do you do your homework now or after dinner?"

Lastly, "Which do you prefer, blue shirts or red shirts?"

Positive Redirection is Tool #2.

When we say negative things to our kids, like "I can't eat ice cream before dinner" or "Stop slamming the door!" as parents, we may not always be conscious of it. In actuality, studies reveal that negative interactions account for 80% of parent-child interactions. Of course, there are instances when you must tell your kids no, but the issue is that if you say no too frequently, it will eventually lose its impact and have a detrimental effect on their confidence and sense of self-worth.

Researchers in psychology have discovered that merely cutting back on the usage of the word "no" and other negative comments and substituting them with more positive options can have a significant impact on a child's motivation and conduct.

Make use of positive redirection.

A. In the event that your child requests anything you'd prefer not to offer them:

1. Begin with a yes response, regardless of whether you approve the request. You can now reroute requests thanks to this. An illustration would be as follows.

• Rather than saying "I can't buy it now," respond to the question "I want this toy" with "Yes, please put it on your birthday list!"

B. If your child wishes you to cease doing something, then:

1. To do this without raising your voice, use a firm, positive command, sometimes referred to as the "start command" (see the example below).

2. Offer substitute activities or approaches, if at all possible. An illustration would be as follows.

•Please refrain from shouting at me. Talk softly.

• Gently pat the dog instead of telling it to "Stop hurting it."

Tool 3: Solving Problems

When our kids act rudely, as parents, we frequently neglect to provide them answers or to enforce consequences and punishments. They deny kids the chance to figure out what's wrong on their own or why they behave the way they do. We undervalue their capacity to resolve issues on their own and deny them the chance to do so by doing this. Rather than emphasizing outcomes and penalties—which could negatively impact motivation—this tool helps kids solve challenges. It's an excellent method of teaching your kids to think independently and accept accountability for their actions. When compared to other forms of discipline, it is significantly more effective.

Applying issue-solving techniques:

There are two ways you can utilize this tool:

1. Your kid is having an issue. Here's the issue: For instance, you don't like school, you don't have any friends, you can't finish your homework by the deadline,

etc. (Note: This is their problem, not yours.)!): a) Pose the question, "What can you do about this?" to your child and help them take responsibility for their issue. Typically, the response to this query is "I don't know." particularly if you've never been "guided" to solve a problem before. You can, therefore, respond to this query. "Do you want me to give you any ideas?" Or alternatively, "Do you want me to tell you what the other kids tried?"

b) If they say no, they say yes, but I always ask here if you decide to alter your mind.

c) Should they respond in the affirmative, kindly consult multiple possibilities for potential resolutions. Please offer a minimum of two options.

d) Self-determination: Encourage your youngster to assess each solution by asking, "How does it work for you?" after you've explained it to them. Say to your child, "Think about it, I'll find out how the other kids handled this problem, and I'll get back to you," if you are at a loss for ideas right away.

a) Express curiosity, but stay out of the way. Tell me what happens to everything when your child chooses the best course of action (either the one you offered or the one they came up with on their own). Good luck to you!"

2. If you would like to talk to your child about an issue you are having, Maybe you want to help them figure out how to solve this issue and work on improving some of their behavior.

a) Begin the process of solving problems. Engaging in activities that kids love is the most efficient way to accomplish this. As an alternative, you might include this activity in your family gathering. Instead of placing the blame on your child for their actions, explain why this isn't working for you and pinpoint the precise issue.

b) Pose a question to your youngster that shows they are taking part in it together. "What shall I do?"

c) Assist your youngster in coming up with potential fixes for issues. Tell me what you can do the next time you spot an issue.

d) Pay close attention to what they propose, and then inquire, "How do you think it will help you?"

e) Arrange brainstorming meetings. Select the greatest answer, in your opinion, and jointly come up with ideas for how to make it happen.

f) Find out from your child how they want to be alerted in the event that they violate your agreement. Help them think of creative methods to remind them if they don't have any ideas of their own.

Putting Limits On Things And Saying No

Establishing and preserving self-esteem requires the ability to set limits and say no. They enable you to put your health first, safeguard your time and energy, and sustain wholesome connections. This chapter will go over a thorough how-to that will help you create boundaries and firmly say no when it's time.

Step 1: Determine Your Needs and Values

Consider your requirements and values carefully. Recognize your priorities and the necessities for preserving your wellbeing. Setting boundaries that uphold your self-esteem and are consistent with your ideals will be made easier by this self-awareness.

Step 2: Recognize the Value of Boundaries

Realize that establishing limits is important for your physical, mental, and emotional wellbeing rather than being selfish. Recognize that by establishing boundaries, you are fostering an environment that is balanced and healthful for both you and the people around you.

Step 3: Express Yourself Clearly and Firmly

Learn to express your boundaries in a strong and clear manner. When expressing your demands and limitations, use "I" statements. Make sure that people know your boundaries by communicating in a straightforward and precise manner.

Step 4: Practice Saying No. Make it a habit to turn down requests or expectations that don't fit with your values or go beyond what you can do. When responding, maintain your composure and assertiveness without feeling obligated to offer lengthy justifications or excuses.

Step 5: Examine Your Options

If it's suitable, think about providing alternatives when expressing no. Make recommendations for substitutes or concessions that will satisfy your requirements and those of others at the same time. This shows that you are willing to work toward solutions that will benefit all parties.

Step 6: Make self-care and wellbeing a priority

Recognize that saying no and establishing boundaries are self-care practices. Make your health a top priority and acknowledge your right to defend your time, energy, and emotional resources. You should respect yourself enough to set limits that uphold your sense of worth.

Step 7: Prepare for and Expect Resistance

Be ready for pushback or opposition when you establish limits or say no. At first, some people might find it difficult to accept your boundaries. Remain steadfast and self-assured in your choice, and be ready to set limits again if needed.

Step 8: Look for Assistance

See a therapist, family member, or trusted friend for support if you find that setting boundaries is difficult or overwhelming. They can offer direction, comfort, and useful counsel on how to set and uphold appropriate boundaries.

Step 9: Engage in introspection

Consider your boundaries often and determine whether they are really supporting your needs. Determine whether any alterations or revisions are required to correspond with your changing requirements and personal development.

Step 10: Respect the Boundaries of Others

As you would like others to respect your boundaries, respect theirs as well. Realize that establishing limits is a mutually beneficial and necessary part of preserving polite and healthy relationships.

Step 11: Honor Your Achievements

Celebrate and acknowledge your success in learning to say no and set boundaries. Acknowledge the beneficial effects it has on your wellbeing and sense of self. Honoring your accomplishments gives you more self-assurance to establish and uphold boundaries.

Establishing boundaries is a lifelong process that calls for assertiveness, self-awareness, and self-care. Accept the importance of saying no and set limits that will boost your self-worth and promote wholesome connections.

Accepting Personal Development

A great method to promote skill development, self-esteem, and personal progress is to embrace self-improvement. It entails a dedication to ongoing development, introspection, and lifelong learning. In this chapter, we'll look at a thorough manual that will assist you in embracing self-improvement and developing a strong feeling of self-worth.

Step 1: Make Specific and Valuable Goals

Establish measurable objectives for your journey toward self-improvement. These objectives must be time-bound, meaningful, quantifiable, achievable, and targeted (SMART). Establishing objectives helps you stay focused and on track, which gives you a sense of accomplishment.

Step 2: Determine Potential Growth and Development Areas

Think about the aspects of your life that you would like to develop and enhance. This could encompass any area of your life that you feel needs attention, whether it is relationships, health, professional knowledge, or personal talents. Finding these regions aids in organizing and focusing your efforts.

Step 3: Learn and Seek Information Constantly

As you pursue your areas of interest and personal development, make a commitment to lifelong learning. Accept that learning is an ongoing and important aspect of your quest for personal development.

Step 4: Accept Input and Introspection

Remain receptive to criticism from others and to introspection. Feedback gives you important information about your areas of strength and growth. Regular self-reflection can help you evaluate your progress, spot trends, and make any necessary corrections.

Step 5: Exercise Consistency and Self-Control

Establish constancy and self-discipline in the pursuit of your personal development objectives. Establish a schedule and commit time and energy to your own development on a regular basis. Taking consistent action gives you momentum and enables you to advance meaningfully over time.

Move Outside of Your Comfort Zone in Step Six

Make it a challenge to leave your comfort zone and open yourself up to new experiences. Growth frequently takes place outside of one's comfort zone. Try new things, take measured chances, and seize chances to broaden your horizons and develop your skills.

Step 7: Develop a Growth Mentality

Adopt a growth mentality that honors the value of perseverance, learning, and hard work. Accept obstacles as chances for personal development and see failures as teaching moments. Beliefs that limit you should be replaced with ones that encourage growth and development.

Step 8: Stress Patience and Self-Compassion

Throughout your self-improvement journey, remember to be patient and kind to yourself. Treat yourself well when you encounter difficulties or failures. Realize that progress requires time and work, and give yourself space to make errors and pick up new skills along the way.

Step 9: Look for Assistance and Responsibility

Assemble a support network that will motivate and hold you responsible for achieving your self-improvement objectives. Tell dependable family members, friends, or mentors about your goals; they can provide support, inspiration, and helpful criticism.

Step 10: Honor accomplishments and advancements

Celebrate your accomplishments and note your advancements as you go. Acknowledge and value the progress you have made in your development. Celebrating accomplishments boosts your self-confidence and inspires you to keep working toward better.

Step 11: Change and Progress

While you're on your path to self-improvement, remain adaptive and flexible. Be willing to modify your objectives, plans, and methods in light of fresh information and evolving situations. Accept the fact that you will be changing and improving as you gain knowledge and experience.

Self-improvement is an ongoing, lifetime endeavor. Seize the chance to grow, learn, and become the greatest version of yourself.

WAYS TO QUIT CONCERNING ONESELF WITH OTHER PEOPLE'S VIEWS

Imagine for once not having to worry about what many people think of you, thoughts that you can never really control anyhow. Isn't that uplifting and liberating? If left unchecked, the tendency to care about other people's opinions can persist indefinitely. It's a major factor in the innumerable dreams that never come true. You have the opportunity to establish a solid, stable foundation for your life as a teenager. Now is the ideal moment to prepare yourself for the worst-case scenarios that may arise. The following details tried-and-true methods for reprogramming your mind to enable you to at last quit worrying about what other people think:

Your perspective can either make life amazing or unnecessarily painful: Whether or not what someone says will have an impact on you depends on how you interpret it. How many of the opinions you worry about now will matter in five months or five years? Consider this. It will be easier for you to see how little of an impact other people's opinions have on your life if you can see the situation from above. Why give other people's opinions so much weight and credit when they can't make your life better or add much worth to it? Your success will always be based on your perception of who you are and how you see yourself. Never let that be your problem; if others don't realize how amazing and valuable you are, then that should be their problem. Accept that no matter how well or poorly you behave, people will always have something to say. Develop the ability to remain focused and resist being influenced by those who don't know you well enough.

Consider the following, introspect, and consider your ideas and beliefs: During your adolescent years, you may hear hurtful and depressing remarks from others. It has the power to sow fears and self-doubt that could prevent you from being your best self every day. Always take the time to ask questions before taking whatever you hear at face value.

Imagine what your peers will probably say about you if they perceive your achievement as a source of jealousy and intimidation. Negative things would be done to you to help you feel less uneasy about yourself by dimming your dazzling light.

They win, and it does you no good at all if you take their advice to heart and start acting in ways that minimize who you are. Find out where their opinions originate. This helps you better comprehend the motivations behind the words and actions of others. The majority of people behave in ways that are a result of acting on their fears and worldviews. Teens who have a hard time liking who they are frequently let down by others and start to believe that everyone else is miserable as well. Don't let the negative opinions and viewpoints of others prevent you from seeing yourself for the actual beauty that you are. Your daily beliefs and thoughts should be ones that will only sprout into the positive outcomes you hope to see.

Give up striving for perfection in favor of effort: It wears you out and teaches others that it's acceptable to have high expectations of yourself when you evaluate yourself too harshly and set unfair standards for yourself. Your teenage years are a time of fast development and limitless possibilities to figure out what really interests you and what suits you best. At this point, you have to give yourself permission to try new things and figure out what doesn't work. Don't see things negatively, even when they rarely go smoothly. Recall that the true definition of failure is staying still and making no effort at all. People will respect you more if they can tell that you don't care what they think of you when you're attempting new things and experiencing disappointment. What's even more intriguing is that by allowing yourself to bravely explore the world, you've inspired others to do the same. You will witness your peers attempt new things without the worry of unjustified criticism from others before you realize it.

Avoid being paralyzed by perfectionism: You can prevent perfectionism from paralyzing you in a number of ways. This is the moment when you feel unprepared to perform an action, and the only way you can fulfill the task is if you are certain that you can perform it flawlessly. This is an incredibly unrealistic objective that will only prevent you from making the essential progress. Which exacerbates feelings of overwhelm and self-dissatisfaction. Learn to accept life as it comes each day. Divide your objectives into manageable to-do lists. Do not deny yourself the pleasure of acknowledging and appreciating each accomplishment along the journey. Appreciate your progress and make it your primary goal. Many people will admire how you treat yourself and adopt a positive outlook when you start to value yourself more. Since you would have taken care of yourself, a lot of people will cease trying to make you perfect.

Know oneself deeply and thoroughly: If you truly believe that you are a kind person, a capable learner, a devoted sibling, and so much more, then this self-awareness ought to serve as your steadfast foundation. If you stay true to your idea of your genuine identity, the winds of erroneous assumptions and views from others about you will have little to no effect. But when you don't know yourself, you can be influenced by what other people think of you. It doesn't matter who you are; you'll be defined by the things others say. Your conscience will tell you that you are not a horrible person, yet you still think that. Spend some time getting to know and love who you are so that it won't matter how much other people say about you.

Establish a significant tribe of your own: There are, however, a few special individuals in your life that you should cherish. People you can turn to for direction and counsel. These individuals may be friends or family members that you know sincerely love you. Make an effort to build a closer bond with them. Enrolling in therapy or hiring a life coach might be important additional sources of assistance. What they think and say can help you grow as a person since they will have your best interests at eart. Maintain close relationships with kind people from whom you can learn at all times. They frequently even know your flaws and strengths, even if you might not be aware of them. Gettin insight from them will surely enable you to obtain the assistance you require to maximize your existence.

Accepting Inner-Directness: Determining Your Natural Strengths

The first part of "How to Become an Empowered Introvert:Embrace Your Quiet Power and Thrive in Every Aspect of Life" is now available for viewing. In this chapter, we will explore the beauty and power of introversion, helping you understand the benefits of being an introvert and accepting your unique features.

Discovering Inner-Directness's Power

It's important to realize that self-preoccupation is a crucial character feature rather than a weakness in a society that often celebrates extroverted traits like confidence and sociability. Self-observers find their energy inward, seeking comfort and healing in moments of being alone. While extroverts flourish in social situations, introverts find strength in solitude, thoughtfulness, and contemplation. Accepting self-preoccupation means realizing that some of history's most fascinating academics, artisans, and trailblazers were born with a gift.

The Characteristics of a Withdrawn Mind

Acknowledging and appreciating the fascinating aspects that go along with introspection is necessary to really embrace it. As keen watchers and listeners, introverts are able to discern nuances that others may overlook. Your ability to think deeply and extensively about information allows you to come up with original solutions and make well-considered conclusions. In a world that moves quickly, having the ability to pause and think things through provides a valuable perspective that can inspire innovative ideas and plans.

Furthermore, self-preoccupation fosters empathy and sympathy. Making meaningful and long-lasting connections is facilitated by your capacity to interact with people on a deep level. Your unique talent for perceiving people's emotions and providing validated assistance is invaluable in both personal and professional contexts. You have the intelligence and compassion to build understanding scaffolds and foster a sense of community.

One of the cornerstones of accepting introversion is realizing the value of quiet time and introspection. Investing energy on its own, contrary to common misconceptions, is most definitely not a sign of limitation or inadequacy. Rather, it is a source of power that enables you to refuel and maximize the creative potential that you possess. Being alone provides a stable environment for deep thought and introspection, enabling you to gain insight into your own opinions, emotions, and desires.

Accepting Who You Really Are

Contemplative persons may be led to believe that they must alter in order to achieve or fit in by the presumptions and conflicts of society. However, accepting self-preoccupation means believing that you are exempt from having to conform to these values. Instead of being a barrier, your inner directness is a superpower that you can use to your advantage. Accepting and appreciating your thinking traits, as well as realizing that they are a fundamental part of who you are, are all part of embracing your credible self.

Adapting to a World of Extroverts: You have to learn how to exist in an extrovert world even as you embrace your introverted personality. This includes realizing that socializing and managing systems could be draining your energy but that you can develop strong interpersonal skills and set boundaries to protect yourself. We will look into several approaches and techniques to help you thrive in social situations while staying true to your contemplative self.

Developing as an Enabled, Thoughtful person

Understanding and embracing your pondering is the most significant move towards turning into an engaged loner and keeping on with a satisfying and real life. In the upcoming sections, we will drill further into specified parts of strengthening, including creating self-assurance, tracking down your passion, framing certified associations, beating social anxiousness, and embracing withdrawn authority.

Embrace your withdrawn assets and set out on an expedition of self-disclosure and self-awareness as we progress with these enabling aids for contemplative persons. Recollect that your self-preoccupation is a strong gift that, when welcomed and sustained, can motivate an existence of realness, success, and significant affiliations.

Your Tone, Accent, And Pace

While you should always be proud of your national or racial history, you need to exercise greater caution in commercial dealings. Slang, colloquialisms, and excessive accent use might make you seem terrible and unfit for some corporate settings. Because there are so many synonyms in the English language, you should have no trouble expressing yourself clearly. When conversing with pals, express yourself using your own language. When you're with friends, you should be able to be yourself without worrying about what other people think. Feel free to be yourself; your accent might make you even more of a standout and respected part of the group.

The social interaction's theme should be reflected in your tone. Whether you're at a bank, a funeral, or a piano concert, loud, high-pitched, and animated vocalizations will be perceived as impolite and will put you in the wrong. In most social circumstances, a dull, plodding, and uninteresting tone will be viewed as boring; therefore, try to maintain your tone more dynamic and engaging. Don't change your frequency until the circumstances call for it. When your friend tells you about their promotion, you should congratulate them more forcefully, but not so much that it looks like you're pretending to be happy about it. Attempt to detect the mood of the circumstance or yourself, as this will usually dictate your tone. Then, attempt to stay true to that feeling.

Speaking at a fast speed can affect the people you converse with. Chatting slowly when chatting with your supervisor could indicate that you are angry with them, your job, or the world in general or that you haven't had your morning coffee yet. Remain positive and adaptable. Steer clear of speaking too quickly and without pausing. Your cognitive process may become confused or complicated as a result of the rushed blunders you start making. Speaking slowly gives listeners more time to assimilate what you're saying. It will make them feel as though you're talking about something fascinating that needs their whole focus. Take advantage of this by speaking more slowly while discussing the points that are crucial for your audience to remember. To keep them on task, speak in a calm tone. Once you've covered the essential points, you can lighten the mood, crack a joke, or get the other person's viewpoint.

The Brain And Emotional Growth

Gaining a deeper understanding of the human mind and its functioning is the first step towards understanding your emotions and the reasons for their behavior. The simplest way to conceptualize the brain is as a computer. Just as a machine has programming, so too are you in charge of the type of code that operates within your mind. The concepts and thoughts you feed your head are the programming that make up your brain.

The recollections you preserve for later use.

The brain is an amazing organ, but it's also a complicated machine that governs every action you take. The brain controls everything, including the smallest movement in your fingers and every breath you take.

Therefore, processing, understanding, and regulating our emotions and subsequent responses are all heavily dependent on the brain. The first step to eventually mastering your emotions is understanding how your mind functions.

Recognizing the Origin

There is a lot going on in your mind. The way your brain interprets emotional situations has a big impact on how you feel after something has happened. The way your brain processes and processes this information determines how you react and feel. You are largely unaware of all of this happening to you. How often have you paused to consider the extent to which my brain affects my emotions?

As was established in Chapter 1, our brain's limbic system is a component of a larger, interconnected structure that controls our emotions and behaviors.

Let's investigate this source a bit more and identify the structures that support the limbic system's general functionality:

The hippocampal region This area of the brain stores and retrieves memories. The hippocampal region also aids in our comprehension and processing of the spatial aspects of our surroundings. This is the area of the brain that serves as a reminder of the appropriate course of action. People with persistent depression will see a decrease in the size of their hippocampal region.

The hypothalamus is the area of the brain responsible for regulating our emotional reactions, hormone release, body temperature, and the sensation of a sexual response.

The amygdala The amygdala is a small brain region, but it has thousands of cell circuits with distinct functions. Bonding, love, sexual behavior, aggression, anger, and fear are the main topics of these circuits. The function of the amygdala is to create an emotional recall of an event or object by giving it an emotional value.

There are both happy and bad memories associated with these feelings. The amygdala facilitates the coordination of our responses to external stimuli. Anger and fear are two of the seven fundamental emotions we feel, and they both heavily depend on it. Researchers studying emotion found in an intriguing study from 1939 that the removal of the amygdala in experimentation caused strange behavior patterns in the monkeys.

The study's conclusions demonstrated that when the monkeys lost their amygdala, they either developed hypersexual tendencies, were fearless or excessively violent, or lost all emotion.

Picture Source: The Health of Your Brain

The Limbic Cortex - The two regions that comprise the limbic cortex are the cingulate gyrus and the para-hippocampal gyrus. Together, these two structures influence our mood, motivation, and judgment.

A few more guidelines

\# Accept responsibility for your own shortcomings and issues. In the same vein, take ownership of your own happiness.

\# Acquire self-love and learn to say no. Enjoy your favorite ritual without feeling guilty.

\# Have huge ideas to achieve greater things.

\# Try not to be too sensitive or irritable. Not every statement is directed at you specifically.

\# Give failures plenty of chances. It's not always unfair in life.

\# Rise to obstacles head-on.

Your Joy Spoilers: Please remove those.

Remove these spoilers from your life and watch as eternal bliss begins to bloom.

Game of Blame

Give up assigning blame; nobody is flawless. You also have some responsibility if the people in your office aren't producing the desired results. Avoid making too many requests too quickly. To achieve perfection, you must learn to accept responsibility.

Selfishness

Those who find admiration in your conceit are shallow. Take care of your character, actions, attitudes, and sincere connections. Don't set meaningless goals for your life.

Uncertainties

When your fears startle you, how can you be content? Your anxieties will cause you to cling to worldly possessions and narrow your viewpoint. Rather, trust in the power of letting go. Have a big heart to feel happy.

Complaining

Your speech has a significant impact on who you are. Unnecessary complaining and whining will only make you feel worse by filling you with negativity. Strive to implement the change and get things functioning. There is hardly anyone who likes a complainer. After a while, even your family and friends will become agitated.

Complaints

It doesn't make you look better to criticize other people. It reveals your narrow-minded, conceited, and arrogant mindset. Everyone works really hard and succeeds in what they do. Recognize and value the individuality of those in your vicinity.

Judging

You never know what kind of life someone else may be leading, so try not to pass judgment.

Overanalyzing

Don't think ahead of time. It won't be of any assistance at all. Thinking too much will take away your tranquility and cause you to put off being happy.

1.1 Talk Formats

A lot of dialogic education strategies, like "Thinking Together," focus primarily on teaching exploratory Talk. As part of a trio of "forms of speaking" (Exploratory Speaking, Disputational Talk, and Cumulative Talk), Douglas Barnes originated the idea of Exploratory Talk in the 1970s, although Neil Mercer primarily developed the version behind Talking Together (Mercer, 1995). However, what precisely is a "talk type"?

The three forms and variations are classified as follows in a number of publications, journals, and blogs:

Dispute Discussion

Disagreement and personalized decision-making characterize discourse. Few efforts are made to share resources, provide helpful criticism, or generate ideas. Debate dialog frequently includes a number of debate-specific characteristics, such as quick exchanges of questions and claims or counter-arguments.

Combined Speech

Communication that incorporates the ideas of others in a positive, nonjudgmental manner is known as cumulative Talk. Through communicating, partners employ aggregation to establish "common knowledge." Collective discourse is characterized by elaborations, affirmations, and repetitions.

Investigative Discussion

In an exploratory talk, partners exchange ideas and engage with one another in a tactful but constructive manner. Comments and recommendations receive equal attention. Those are debatable, but criticisms are legitimate, and competing hypotheses are put forth. Before reaching a conclusion as a group, partners actively participate, and their opinions are heard and considered. In contrast to the other two formats, the Talk's reasoning is clearer, and information is held more accountable to the public in the Exploratory Talk.

Perhaps talk forms can accomplish more than just a coding system. They sense a youngster's excitement instantly rather than measuring the curve of their smile and comparing it to the look in their eyes to determine whether or not the child is grinning.

Similarly, in order to determine whether or not a community is functioning successfully, teachers don't always need to collect and code "info" discourse.

Additionally appropriate are the mannerisms, body language, and tone of voice. Disputation Talk is when problems are discussed without clarification or understanding, and you have to step in to resolve them. You should probably end the conversation if the vocabulary and body language show a shared dedication. This is known as exploratory conversation. This approach to watching Talk in action in a busy classroom depends on the teacher's willingness to participate in the conversations among the students, understanding what is actually going on between them in ways that aren't always immediately conveyed through the words spoken.

1.2 Motivation to Speak

Why do experts recommend talking after a disaster, regardless of how big, little, personal, or global the issue maybe? Since it is a part of our innate, holistic healing skills. We communicate our needs and wants with words, and our feelings need to follow suit. When we're children, for example, we notify our parents when anything is wrong with words so they may console us and put things right. As adults, this doesn't change. Speaking with someone can be quite beneficial, particularly if the trauma or problem is persistent, unanticipated, or lacks an easy fix.

Even though the discussion might seem unimportant, it's crucial to lead a healthy lifestyle and experience a range of emotions. Contact is effective for improving mental health, whether it is by discussing concerns you have or just having a general talk. You can converse with others more for the following reasons!

Reduces Stress

It is very beneficial to talk about a problem you are facing in order to relieve some of your tension and give your ideas a voice. Studies show that doing good deeds triggers the release of stress-relieving chemicals. Additionally, healthy relationships promote emotional stability and well-being, both of which reduce stress.

Even if all of your issues may be internal, it might be difficult to accept this. However, once you state the obvious, it becomes simpler to grasp the issues.

Your problems frequently appear greater and bigger than they actually are if you're thinking about them all the time without discussing them with anyone. You may trim someone down to size by speaking with them. If something annoys you, someone who doesn't care about it might provide some alternatives you hadn't considered.

Enhances Interactions

You can enhance your relationship with those around you by getting to know them better through increased conversation. Numerous studies have demonstrated that it is simpler for those who live longer, have fewer health problems, and have satisfying interactions with others. Conversely, problems such as depression are associated with a deficiency of social ties.

Someone who is concerned yet neutral won't take sides or forward any agenda when you chat with them. Speaking is like having a head pressure valve that you can occasionally turn on. Choosing the person you want to speak with is a crucial first step. The fact that you can trust the individual you wish to speak with, though, maybe even more crucial.

This provides us with a feeling of something to "do." By chatting, we're making a connection and being proactive rather than passive.

www.ingramcontent.com/pod-product-compliance
Lightning Source LLC
Chambersburg PA
CBHW052133110526
44591CB00012B/1702